ITALIAN

© 1998 Rebo International b.v., Lisse. The Netherlands
1998 Published by Rebo Productions Ltd., London
Designed and created by Consortium, England

Original recipes and photographs © Ceres Verlag,
Rudolf-August Oetker KG, Bielefeld

Typeset by MATS, Southend-on-Sea, Essex
Printed in Slovenia
Edited by Anne Sheasby
Recipes compiled and translated by
Stephen Challacombe
Illustrations by Camilla Sopwith

ISBN 184053 083 9

Italian

Classic and contemporary dishes
to enjoy every day

REBO
PRODUCTIONS

Contents

Introduction

One of the most popular cuisines in the world, Italian cooking offers a wealth of variety in its traditional dishes for everyone to enjoy. This variety stems from its ancient and colourful heritage, from Greek, Roman, Byzantine and even Oriental origins. Culinary traditions in Italy are also intensely regional, and this serves to perpetuate the wide range of cooking skills and specialities drawn from every part of the country.

The combination of the use of good-quality, fresh ingredients and easy, often quick cooking methods ensures the ever-growing appeal of Italian cookery in today's health and time-conscious world. Italian food offers a healthy option for everyday eating, with its emphasis on olive oil rather than saturated, animal fats for cooking; boiled pasta and rice, and bread as accompaniments rather than potatoes cooked in oil; and large quantities and a rich variety of fresh vegetables and herbs combined with relatively small servings of meat or fish.

This book offers a selection of classic and contemporary Italian dishes for a variety of occasions – for satisfying family meals, special occasions and entertaining, as well as for alfresco lunches and comforting suppers. For maximum flavour and authenticity, use the specific Italian ingredients where given in the recipes rather than using substitutes, for example risotto rice, freshly grated Parmesan cheese and Parma ham.

Minestrone

A delicious and filling version of the classic Italian soup, thickened with rice rather than the traditional pasta.

Preparation time: 12 hours soaking time, plus 1-1½ hours pre-cooking • Cooking time: 1 hour • Serves: 6-8

Ingredients

150 g (5½ oz) borlotti or dried white beans	*2 leeks, cut lengthways and sliced*
60 ml (4 tbsp) olive oil	*1 bay leaf*
100 g (3½ oz) streaky bacon, diced	*15 ml (1 tbsp) chopped fresh basil*
1 onion, chopped	*2 litres (3½ pints) vegetable stock*
2 cloves garlic, crushed	*150 g (5½ oz) long-grain white rice*
250 g (9 oz) floury potatoes, diced	*250 g (9 oz) tomatoes, skinned and quartered*
250 g (9 oz) carrots, sliced	*200 g (7 oz) frozen peas*
350 g (12 oz) courgettes, sliced	*Salt and freshly ground black pepper*
2 sticks celery, chopped	*Freshly grated Parmesan cheese, to serve*

Method

1

Soak the beans in a bowl of cold water for 12 hours. Drain the beans, place them in a large saucepan and cover with fresh water. Cover, bring to the boil and simmer for 1-1½ hours, or until cooked. Drain thoroughly, discarding the water.

2

Heat the oil in a saucepan, add the bacon, onion and garlic and cook for about 10 minutes, or until the onion is softened, stirring occasionally. Add the potatoes, carrots, courgettes, celery, leeks, bay leaf and basil and cook for 5 minutes, stirring occasionally.

3

Add the stock and cooked beans and stir to mix. Cover, bring to the boil, then simmer for 25 minutes, stirring occasionally.

4

Remove and discard the bay leaf, stir in the rice, then cover and simmer for 15 minutes, stirring occasionally.

5

Add the tomatoes and peas and cook for a further 5 minutes, or until the rice and vegetables are cooked and tender, stirring occasionally. Season with salt and pepper. Ladle into warmed soup bowls to serve and sprinkle with Parmesan cheese.

Serving suggestion
Serve with fresh crusty bread or toast.

Variations
Use swede or turnip in place of the carrot. Use sweet potatoes in place of the standard potatoes.

Cook's tip
A quick and easy way to skin tomatoes is to cut a small cross on the base of each tomato. Place the tomatoes in boiling water for 10-15 seconds. Transfer to a bowl of cold water using a slotted spoon. Lift out and remove the skins. Use as required.

Mixed Fish Soup

A flavourful fish soup containing a variety of fresh fish and shellfish including mussels, squid and prawns.

Preparation time: 45 minutes • Cooking time: 1¼ hours • Serves: 6-8

Ingredients

1 kg (2 lb 4 oz) mussels	1 head of celery, chopped
120 ml (8 tbsp) olive oil	1 clove garlic, crushed
2 kg (4 lb 8 oz) whole fish such as hake, sole, turbot, eel and cod	1 red pepper, seeded and finely chopped
	15-30 ml (1-2 tbsp) chopped fresh thyme
Juice of 2 lemons	250 ml (9 fl oz) dry white wine
300 g (10½ oz) prepared squid	Salt and freshly ground black pepper
1 onion, finely chopped	12 king prawns, peeled
4 tomatoes, skinned and quartered	6-8 small slices white bread, crusts removed, each cut into a round
1 carrot, sliced	

Method

1

Fill the sink with cold water, add the mussels and swirl around. If the water becomes sandy or cloudy, drain the sink and repeat the process until the water remains clear.

2

Scrub the mussels with a clean hard brush, discarding any mussels that are broken or do not close quickly when given a sharp tap. Rinse under cold running water.

3

Heat 45 ml (3 tbsp) oil in a saucepan and add the mussels. Cook for about 5 minutes or until the mussels open, discarding any that do not open. Remove from the pan, then remove the mussels from their shells and set aside. Reserve the cooking juices.

4

Wash the fish and pat dry on kitchen paper. Fillet the fish, removing and reserving the heads, tails, fins, etc. Cut the flesh into bite-sized pieces and set aside.

5

Place the fish tails, heads, etc., in a saucepan with 2 litres (3½ pints) water. Cover, bring to the boil and simmer for 15 minutes. Strain the fish and stock, retaining the stock and discarding the fish heads, etc.

6

Wash and dry the squid and cut into rings. Set aside. Heat 45 ml (3 tbsp) oil in a saucepan and add the onion, tomatoes, carrot, celery, garlic, red pepper and thyme and cook gently for 5 minutes, stirring occasionally.

7

Add the wine and salt and pepper, cover, bring to the boil and simmer for 10 minutes.

8

Add the reserved cooking liquid from the mussels and fish stock, bring to the boil and cook for a further 10 minutes.

9

Add the squid and cook for 10 minutes, then add the fish and prawns and cook for a further 15 minutes, stirring occasionally.

10

Add the mussels and cook for 5 minutes, or until the fish and vegetables are cooked and tender.

11

Meanwhile, heat the remaining oil in a frying pan and fry the bread slices on both sides until golden brown and crisp.

12

To serve, place each fried bread round into the base of a warmed soup bowl and ladle the soup on top.

Serving suggestion
Sprinkle with grated fresh Parmesan cheese just before serving, if liked.

Country Vegetable Soup

A chunky vegetable soup which should be made with the freshest vegetables you can find. Italian cooks vary the vegetables used according to what is in season.

Preparation time: 10 minutes • Cooking time: 35 minutes • Serves: 4-6

Ingredients

30 ml (2 tbsp) olive oil

1 onion, sliced

1 leek, sliced

1 clove garlic, crushed

1 small cauliflower, broken into small florets

400 g (14 oz) broccoli, broken into small florets and stalks sliced

4 medium-sized carrots, sliced

200 g (7 oz) celeriac, cut into chunks

3 beefsteak tomatoes, skinned and quartered

1.2 litres (2 pints) vegetable stock

Salt and freshly ground black pepper

Chopped fresh parsley, to serve

Method

1
Heat the oil in a saucepan. Add the onion, leek and garlic and cook for about 10 minutes, or until the onion is softened, stirring occasionally.

2
Add the cauliflower, broccoli, carrots and celeriac and cook for 5 minutes, stirring occasionally.

3
Add the tomatoes, stock and salt and pepper to taste and stir to mix. Cover, bring to the boil, then simmer for 20 minutes, stirring occasionally, until the vegetables are cooked and tender.

4
Check the seasoning, then ladle into warmed soup bowls. Sprinkle with chopped fresh parsley before serving.

Serving suggestion
Serve with warm, fresh country-style Italian bread.

Variations
Use a mixture of parsnip and swede in place of the celeriac. If available, add 5 ml (1 tsp) chopped fresh marjoram and 5 ml (1 tsp) chopped fresh thyme with the tomatoes and stock, for extra flavour. To make a smooth-textured soup, allow the cooked soup to cool, then purée in a food processor. Return to the saucepan and reheat gently.

Beef Soup with Meatballs

A tasty addition to a simple beef stock, the meatballs in this recipe combine minced beef and spinach with a touch of Parmesan cheese.

Preparation time: 30 minutes • Cooking time: 10-20 minutes • Serves: 6

Ingredients

200 g (7 oz) fresh spinach leaves	*15 ml (1 tbsp) butter, softened*
25 g (1 oz) lard	*3 medium eggs, beaten*
200 g (7 oz) minced beef	*Salt and freshly ground black pepper*
55 g (2 oz) fresh Parmesan cheese, grated	*2 litres (3½ pints) beef stock, preferably home-made*
55 g (2 oz) fresh white breadcrumbs	

Method

1

Rinse the spinach leaves under cold running water and place them in a saucepan with no additional water. Cover and cook gently for 5-10 minutes, or until the spinach is wilted and cooked, shaking the pan occasionally.

2

Drain the spinach thoroughly, pressing any excess water out of the spinach using the back of a wooden spoon. Chop finely.

3

Place the spinach in a bowl, add the lard, minced beef, Parmesan cheese, breadcrumbs, butter, eggs and seasoning and mix thoroughly.

4

Form the mince mixture into small meatballs.

5

Pour the stock into a saucepan and bring to the boil. Using a slotted spoon, add the meatballs to the boiling stock.

6

Cover, bring to the boil, then cook gently for 5-10 minutes, or until the meatballs are thoroughly cooked. Ladle into warmed soup bowls to serve.

Serving suggestion

Serve with toasted croutons or thick slices of fresh crusty bread.

Variations

Use lamb or chicken mince and stock in place of the beef. Use spring greens in place of the spinach. Use brown or wholemeal breadcrumbs in place of the white breadcrumbs.

Cook's tips

To make a simple home-made beef stock, brown some meat bones in the oven, then place them in a saucepan with 1 sliced onion, 1 sliced carrot, 1 sliced celery stick, a few fresh herb sprigs and seasoning. Cover with plenty of water, bring to the boil and simmer for 2 hours, skimming occasionally. Strain the stock and when cold, remove and discard the fat. Use as required.

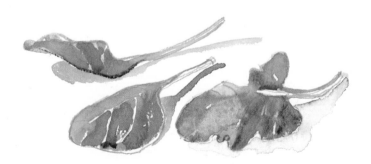

Baked Mussels

An inviting appetizer of crispy-topped, herb-flavoured mussels.

Preparation time: 20 minutes • Cooking time: 8 minutes • Serves: 6-8

Ingredients

1.5 kg (3 lb 5 oz) fresh mussels in their shells, cleaned	*45 ml (3 tbsp) fresh white breadcrumbs*
	Salt and freshly ground black pepper
3 cloves garlic, crushed	*100 g (3½ oz) butter*
2 small shallots, finely chopped	*Juice of 1 lemon*
1 bunch fresh parsley, finely chopped	*Fresh herb sprigs, to garnish*

Method

1

Cook the mussels in a saucepan of boiling water for about 8 minutes, or until their shells open. Discard any mussels that do not open.

2

Remove and discard half the shell of each cooked mussel, leaving the mussel in the other half, and lay them onto a lightly greased baking sheet.

3

Place the garlic, shallots, parsley and breadcrumbs in a blender or food processor and blend until smooth and well mixed. Season to taste with salt and pepper.

4

Spoon a little of the blended mixture onto each mussel.

5

Melt the butter in a saucepan, then drizzle it over the mussels. Sprinkle the lemon juice over the top.

6

Bake in a preheated oven at 200°C/400°F/gas mark 6 for about 8 minutes, or until cooked and bubbling. Serve immediately, garnished with fresh herb sprigs.

Serving suggestion
Serve with a mixed leaf side salad and focaccia bread.

Variations
Use lime juice or orange juice in place of the lemon juice. Use chopped fresh mixed herbs or chives in place of the parsley.

Parma Ham with Melon

A classic and popular dish, this simple and delicious starter will impress your dinner guests.

Preparation time: 20 minutes, plus 2 hours chilling time • Serves: 6

Ingredients

2 honeydew melons	*Freshly ground black pepper*
12 thin slices Parma ham	*Fresh herb sprigs, to garnish*

Method

1
Chill the melon in the refrigerator for about 2 hours before preparing and serving.

2
To prepare the melons, cut each one in half and remove and discard the seeds.

3
Cut each melon half into 3 even wedges or portions and place on a plate. Roll each slice of ham into a roll and sprinkle with freshly ground black pepper.

4
Serve two wedges of melon and 2 rolls of ham per portion.

5
Alternatively, scoop the melon flesh into balls using a melon baller. Divide the melon balls evenly between 6 serving dishes or plates and top each serving with 2 slices of ham. Sprinkle with freshly ground black pepper and serve. Garnish with fresh herb sprigs.

Serving suggestion
Drizzle the melon with a little port or ginger wine just before serving.

Variations
Use other types of melon such as galia or cantaloupe melons or a mixture of two melons in place of the honeydew. Sprinkle the melon with a little ground ginger before serving.

Cook's tip
When buying melons, choose firm fruit which has no visible soft patches or cracks. Melons should feel heavy for their size and most smell fragrant when ripe.

Stuffed Mushrooms

A quick and tasty starter, these stuffed mushrooms also make an ideal snack or supper dish.

Preparation time: 25 minutes • Cooking time: 10 minutes • Serves: 6-8

Ingredients

1 kg (2 lb 4 oz) large field mushrooms	*3 cloves garlic, crushed*
15-30 ml (1-2 tbsp) butter	*Salt and freshly ground black pepper*
1 bunch fresh parsley, finely chopped	*75 ml (5 tbsp) olive oil*
15 ml (1 tbsp) fresh white breadcrumbs	*Fresh herb sprigs, to garnish*

Method

1

Wipe the mushrooms clean, remove the stalks and chop them finely.

2

Melt the butter in a saucepan, add the chopped mushroom stalks and cook over a high heat for 5-10 minutes, or until all the liquid has evaporated, stirring frequently. Remove the pan from the heat.

3

Add the parsley, breadcrumbs, garlic and seasoning and mix well.

4

Spoon the mixture into the mushrooms, dividing it evenly between each one.

5

Place the stuffed mushrooms on a lightly greased baking sheet. Drizzle some oil over each mushroom.

6

Bake in a preheated oven at 200°C/400°F/gas mark 6 for about 10 minutes, or until cooked. Serve immediately, garnished with fresh herb sprigs.

Serving suggestion

Serve with thick slices of fresh Ciabatta bread.

Variations

Use chopped fresh basil in place of the parsley. Use 2 finely chopped shallots in place of the garlic.

Asparagus Imperial

A special way of serving fresh asparagus, in a rich and creamy sauce.

Preparation time: 15 minutes • Cooking time: 20 minutes • Serves: 4

Ingredients

1 kg (2 lb 4 oz) fresh asparagus, trimmed	*2 egg yolks*
15 ml (1 tbsp) butter	*5 ml (1 tsp) cornflour*
15 ml (1 tbsp) caster sugar	*Salt and freshly ground black pepper*
125 ml (4 fl oz) white wine	*150 g (5½ oz) crème fraîche*
	Chopped fresh parsley, to garnish

Method

1

Place the asparagus in a saucepan with the butter and sugar. Cover with boiling water, then return to the boil, cover and simmer for about 20 minutes, until tender. Drain thoroughly and set aside to cool.

2

To make the sauce, place the wine, egg yolks, cornflour and seasoning in a pan. Heat gently, whisking continuously, until the sauce thickens.

3

Remove the pan from the heat, but continue to stir it as it cools.

4

Fold in the crème fraîche and adjust the seasoning.

5

Arrange the asparagus on 4 serving plates and pour the dressing over the top or spoon it alongside. Sprinkle with chopped parsley and serve immediately.

Serving suggestion

Serve with fingers of buttered bread or toast and slices of Parma ham.

Variation

Serve the sauce with other cooked vegetables such as baby courgettes or French beans.

Cook's tip

When buying asparagus, select straight, plump, even stalks with tightly-budded, compact heads. Store in the refrigerator for up to 2 days.

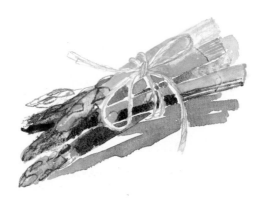

Corsican Tomato Salad

A quick and easy salad to prepare. Serve with fresh crusty bread for a filling starter.

Preparation time: 15 minutes • Serves: 6

Ingredients

6 beefsteak tomatoes	*1 bunch fresh parsley, finely chopped*
2 onions, chopped	*Salt and freshly ground black pepper*
4 cloves garlic, thinly sliced	*60 ml (4 tbsp) olive oil*
45 ml (3 tbsp) capers	*Slices of fresh or preserved goat's cheese, to garnish*
10 black olives	

Method

1

Cut out and discard the core from each tomato.

2

Slice the tomatoes and arrange on a serving plate or platter.

3

Place the onions, garlic, capers, olives, parsley and seasoning in a bowl and stir to mix.

4

Scatter the onion mixture over the tomatoes and drizzle the oil over the top.

5

Serve immediately, garnished with slices of fresh or preserved goat's cheese.

Serving suggestion

Serve with thick slices of Focaccia bread.

Variations

Use large plum tomatoes in place of the beefsteak tomatoes. Use 8 shallots in place of the onions.

Cook's tip

A quick and easy way to chop fresh parsley is to put the parsley into a mug or jug. Using a pair of clean kitchen scissors, cut the parsley up into small pieces.

Asparagus Salad

A delicious asparagus and egg salad which makes an ideal summer lunch or supper dish. Also creates a tasty starter.

Preparation time: 15 minutes • Cooking time: 15 minutes • Serves: 4

Ingredients

500 g (1 lb 2 oz) green and white asparagus, chopped	*15 ml (1 tbsp) white wine vinegar*
5 ml (1 tsp) butter	*15 ml (1 tbsp) lemon juice*
5 ml (1 tsp) salt	*Salt and freshly ground black pepper*
5 ml (1 tsp) caster sugar	*2 medium eggs, hard-boiled*
1 shallot, finely chopped	*30 ml (2 tbsp) chopped fresh parsley*
75 ml (5 tbsp) sunflower oil	*1 lettuce*
	Fresh herb sprigs, to garnish

Method

1
Place the asparagus in a saucepan with the butter, 5 ml (1 tsp) salt and sugar and cover with boiling water.

2
Cover, bring to the boil, then cook gently for 15 minutes, until cooked and tender. Drain thoroughly and keep warm.

3
Place the shallot, oil, vinegar, lemon juice and seasoning in a bowl and whisk together until thoroughly mixed. Adjust the seasoning to taste.

4
Slice the eggs thinly, then gently stir the eggs, asparagus and parsley together to mix.

5
Shred the lettuce, arrange it on 4 serving plates and spoon the asparagus mixture over the beds of lettuce. Drizzle the oil dressing over the top and serve immediately, garnished with fresh herb sprigs.

Serving suggestion
Serve with slices of warm, fresh country-style bread.

Variations
Cook other vegetables such as baby sweetcorn or courgettes in place of the asparagus.
Use chopped fresh chives or basil in place of the parsley.

Ligurian Salad

A classic Italian dish from Liguria which is best made some time in advance of the meal.

Preparation time: 15 minutes, plus 2 hours chilling time • Serves: 4

Ingredients

4 tomatoes	*3 cloves garlic, finely chopped*
2 fresh green chillies	*15 ml (1 tbsp) chopped fresh basil*
½ cucumber	*Salt and freshly ground black pepper*
115 g (4 oz) carrots	*60 ml (4 tbsp) olive oil*
10 silver onions or baby onions	*30 ml (2 tbsp) white wine vinegar*
10 pitted black olives	*Lettuce leaves, to serve*
2 anchovy fillets, chopped	

Method

1

Slice the tomatoes and place in a bowl. Halve and seed the chillies and slice into long thin strips. Add to the tomatoes.

2

Peel, seed and dice the cucumber and cut the carrots into thin strips. Add to the tomatoes.

3

Add the onions, olives, anchovy fillets, garlic, basil and seasoning and stir to mix.

4

Place the oil and vinegar in a small bowl and whisk together. Drizzle over the salad ingredients and toss together to mix.

5

Cover and chill in the refrigerator for at least 2 hours before serving. Serve on a bed of lettuce leaves.

Serving suggestion

Serve with fresh Formaggio bread.

Variations

Use plum or yellow tomatoes or a mixture in place of the standard tomatoes.
Use courgettes in place of the carrots.

Cook's tip

A quick and easy way to make salad dressings is to place all the salad dressing ingredients into a clean screw-top jar.
Screw the lid on and shake until thoroughly mixed. Store in the refrigerator.

Tuna Salad

A simple salad, ideal for a light summer lunch alfresco. Also good served as a starter.

Preparation time: 15 minutes, plus 1 hour chilling time • Serves: 4

Ingredients

1 lettuce	*125 ml (4 fl oz) olive oil*
500g (1 lb 2 oz) tuna canned in brine or oil, drained weight	*Juice of 1 lemon*
1 red onion	*Salt and freshly ground black pepper*
55 g (2 oz) capers	*Fresh dill sprigs, to garnish*

Method

1

Shred the lettuce and arrange it on 4 serving plates. Flake the tuna and spoon it over the lettuce.

2

Thinly slice the onion into rings and arrange them over the tuna. Scatter the capers over the top.

3

Place the oil, lemon juice and seasoning in a bowl and whisk together until well mixed.

4

Drizzle the dressing over the salads.

5

Cover and chill the salads in the refrigerator for 1 hour before serving. Garnish with fresh dill sprigs before serving.

Serving suggestion

Serve with thick slices of fresh country-style Italian bread. Sprinkle the salads with toasted sesame seeds just before serving, if liked.

Variations

Use canned salmon or crab in place of the tuna. Use lime or orange juice in place of the lemon juice for the dressing.

Cook's tip

Capers are generally bottled in brine or vinegar but can also be found salted. Capers should always be rinsed before using to remove excess salt.

Avocado and Spinach Salad

A delicious combination of fresh spinach and avocado, topped with crispy diced bacon.

Preparation time: 15 minutes • Cooking time: 4 minutes • Serves: 4

Ingredients

55 g (2 oz) lean back bacon rashers

300 g (10½ oz) fresh spinach leaves

1 ripe avocado

115g (4 oz) mushrooms

30 ml (2 tbsp) lemon juice

75 ml (5 tbsp) olive oil

5ml (1 tsp) white wine vinegar

A pinch of sugar

Salt and freshly ground black pepper

Method

1

Grill the bacon under a preheated grill for a few minutes on each side, until cooked and crispy, turning occasionally. Set aside to cool, then dice.

2

Wash and drain the spinach leaves and arrange them on 4 serving plates.

3

Halve the avocado, remove the stone, then peel and cut the flesh into thin slices. Arrange over the spinach leaves.

4

Thinly slice the mushrooms and scatter over the avocado. Sprinkle with some of the lemon juice.

5

Place the remaining lemon juice, oil, vinegar, sugar and seasoning in a bowl and whisk together until well mixed.

6

Drizzle the dressing over the salads, toss together to mix, then sprinkle with diced bacon. Serve immediately.

Serving suggestion
Serve with warmed Ciabatta bread.

Variations
Use smoked bacon in place of unsmoked bacon for a tasty alternative. Use baby spinach leaves for the salad, if available. Use wild mushrooms in place of the standard mushrooms.

Cook's tip
A quick way to dice bacon is to use a pair of clean kitchen scissors and snip the bacon into small pieces.

Tuscan Cannelloni

Cannelloni cases are filled with a tasty meat filling to create this popular Tuscan dish.

Preparation time: 2 hours • Cooking time: 30-40 minutes • Serves: 4-6

Ingredients

500 g (1 lb 2 oz) minced beef	200 g (7 oz) fresh Parmesan cheese, grated
350 g (12 oz) plain flour	Freshly ground black pepper
8 medium eggs	125 ml (4 fl oz) white wine
2.5 ml (½ tsp) olive oil	115 g (4 oz) butter
2.5 ml (½ tsp) salt	Fresh herb sprigs, to garnish
200 g (7 oz) chicken livers	

Method

1

Place the minced beef in a saucepan and cover with water. Cover, bring to the boil and simmer for about 1½ hours, or until cooked. Drain and set aside.

2

Meanwhile, make the cannelloni. Sift the flour onto a clean working surface. Make a hollow in the centre of the flour and place 4 eggs, oil and salt in the hollow.

3

Gradually work the ingredients together using both hands, to form a smooth dough.
Cover with a damp tea-towel and leave to rest for 30 minutes.

4

Divide the dough into manageable portions and roll each piece out into a thin rectangle. Leave to dry for 10 minutes.

5

Cook the cannelloni sheets in a large saucepan of lightly salted, boiling water for about 11 minutes, or until al dente. Drain and set aside.

6

Place the cooked mince in a blender or food processor with the chicken livers, remaining 4 eggs, 150 g (5½ oz) Parmesan cheese, black pepper and wine. Blend until smooth.

7

Spoon the blended meat mixture onto the cooked pasta sheets and roll each one up.

8

Place the cannelloni in a lightly greased baking tin or ovenproof dish and dot with butter.
Sprinkle the remaining Parmesan over the top.

9

Bake in a preheated oven at 180°C/350°F/gas mark 4 for 30-40 minutes, or until golden brown.
Serve, garnished with fresh herb sprigs.

Serving suggestion
Serve with cooked seasonal fresh vegetables, such as broccoli florets and baby carrots.

Variations
Use minced lamb or pork in place of the beef. Use red wine or stock in place of the white wine.

Genoan Spaghetti

A tasty pasta dish combining a herby, cheese sauce with freshly cooked pasta.

Preparation time: 15 minutes • Cooking time: 10-12 minutes • Serves: 4

Ingredients

55 g (2 oz) fresh Parmesan cheese, grated	*30 ml (2 tbsp) chopped fresh basil*
70 g (2½ oz) Pecorino (Italian goat's cheese)	*5 ml (1 tsp) salt*
	150 ml (¼ pint) olive oil
5 cloves garlic, crushed	*600 g (1 lb 5 oz) spaghetti*
60 ml (4 tbsp) chopped fresh parsley	*Fresh herb sprigs, to garnish*

Method

1

Place the Parmesan cheese, Pecorino, garlic, parsley, basil and salt in a bowl and mix well.

2

Gradually add the oil, 15 ml (1 tbsp) at a time, to form a creamy mixture. This can also be done in a blender or food processor. Set aside.

3

Cook the spaghetti in a large saucepan of lightly salted, boiling water for 10-12 minutes, or until just cooked and firm to the bite or al dente.

4

Drain the spaghetti and place it in a warmed serving dish.

5

Pour the sauce over the spaghetti, toss together to mix and serve immediately. Sprinkle with a little extra grated Parmesan cheese, before serving, if liked. Garnish with fresh herb sprigs.

Serving suggestion
Serve with crusty French bread.

Variation
Serve the herby cheese sauce with other types of cooked pasta such as tagliatelle or fettucine.

Turkey Pasta Bow Salad

This pasta salad can also be made using chicken or duck in place of the turkey.

Preparation time: 20 minutes, plus cooling time • Cooking time: 15 minutes • Serves: 4

Ingredients

250 g (9 oz) farfalle (pasta bows)	45 ml (3 tbsp) mayonnaise
45 ml (3 tbsp) olive oil	150 g (5½ oz) pot plain yogurt
300 g (10½ oz) turkey breast fillets, cut into thin strips	60 ml (4 tbsp) whipped cream
Salt and freshly ground black pepper	45 ml (3 tbsp) tomato ketchup
4 tomatoes, skinned and sliced	30 ml (2 tbsp) cream sherry or port
300 g (10½ oz) frozen peas, thawed	2.5 ml (½ tsp) caster sugar

Method

1

Cook the farfalle in a large saucepan of lightly salted, boiling water with 15 ml (1 tbsp) oil added for about 11 minutes, or until cooked al dente. Drain thoroughly and set aside to cool.

2

Heat the remaining oil in a frying pan, add the turkey and cook for about 5 minutes, until cooked and tender, stirring frequently. Season with salt and pepper, then set aside to cool.

3

Place the cooled pasta in a bowl, add the turkey, tomatoes and peas and stir to mix.

4

In a separate bowl, mix the mayonnaise, yogurt, cream, tomato ketchup, sherry or port and sugar together until thoroughly mixed. Season to taste with salt and pepper.

5

Spoon the dressing over the pasta mixture and toss together to mix. Serve immediately.

Serving suggestion
Serve with a mixed leaf side salad.

Variations
Use chicken or duck in place of the turkey. Use drained, canned sweetcorn kernels in place of the peas. Use crème fraîche in place of the cream.

Cook's tip
For a warm salad, simply combine the hot pasta and turkey with the other salad ingredients and dressing and serve warm.

Ravioli

A classic recipe, this delicious, authentic Italian ravioli will be enjoyed by all the family.

Preparation time: 50 minutes • Cooking time: 8-10 minutes • Serves: 4-6

Ingredients

For the pasta dough

300 g (10½ oz) plain flour

2 medium eggs, plus 2 egg whites

30 ml (2 tbsp) olive oil

For the filling

30 ml (2 tbsp) olive oil

125 g (4½ oz) minced pork

125 g (4½ oz) minced beef

1 small onion, finely chopped

1 clove garlic, crushed

1 medium carrot, grated

2 egg yolks

15 ml (1 tbsp) tomato purée

1.25 ml (¼ tsp) chopped fresh thyme

Salt and freshly ground black pepper

55 g (2 oz) butter

150 g (5½ oz) fresh Parmesan cheese, grated

30 ml (2 tbsp) chopped fresh parsley,
to garnish

Method

1

To make the pasta dough, sift the flour onto a clean work surface and form a hollow in the centre.

2

Place the eggs, egg whites and 15 ml (1 tbsp) oil in the hollow and, using both hands, knead the ingredients together to form a smooth dough. Cover with a damp tea-towel and leave to rest for 10 minutes.

3

Meanwhile, make the filling. Heat the oil in a saucepan, add the minced meats, onion, garlic and carrot and cook for 5 minutes, stirring occasionally. Remove the pan from the heat.

4

Stir in the egg yolks, tomato purée, thyme and seasoning and mix well.

5

Divide the pasta dough in half and on a lightly floured surface, roll one half out to form a rectangle about 48 x 35 cm (19 x 14 in). Cut the rectangle lengthways into two pieces. Cover one rectangle with a damp tea-towel.

6

Place walnut-sized lumps of the filling mixture onto the other rectangle, placing them about 6 cm (2½ in) apart.

7

With a pastry brush dipped in water, mark a wet line between the heaps of filling. Place the other rectangle on top and press the edges and around the filling together to seal.

8

Using a pastry cutter, cut around the filling to form ravioli and place them on greaseproof paper. Repeat with the remaining dough and filling.

9

Bring a large saucepan of lightly salted water to the boil and add the remaining oil. Cook the ravioli in the boiling water for 8-10 minutes, or until cooked and tender. Drain thoroughly and place on a warmed serving plate.

10

Dot the ravioli with butter, sprinkle with Parmesan cheese and garnish with chopped fresh parsley. Serve immediately.

Serving suggestion

Serve with fresh tomato sauce.

Variations

Use minced turkey and chicken in place of the pork and beef. Use 1 small leek in place of the onion. Use 1 courgette in place of the carrot.

Seafood Tagliatelle

This tasty dish combines mussels and shrimps in a wine sauce served with tagliatelle.

Preparation time: 20 minutes • Cooking time: 15 minutes • Serves: 4

Ingredients

400 g (14 oz) tagliatelle	Salt and freshly ground black pepper
30-45 ml (2-3 tbsp) butter, melted	300 g (10½ oz) frozen mussels in their shells
15 ml (1 tbsp) olive oil	115 g (4 oz) potted or fresh shrimps
1 onion, thinly sliced	500 g (1 lb 2 oz) tomatoes, skinned, seeded and chopped
1 clove garlic, thinly sliced	
125 ml (4 fl oz) white wine	15 ml (1 tbsp) capers
1 bay leaf	30 ml (2 tbsp) chopped fresh parsley

Method

1

Cook the tagliatelle in a large saucepan of lightly salted, boiling water for 8-10 minutes, or until cooked al dente, stirring occasionally. Drain thoroughly, rinse with cold water and drain again.

2

Stir the butter into the pasta and mix well. Keep warm.

3

Heat the oil in a saucepan, add the onion and garlic and cook for 5 minutes, stirring occasionally.

4

Add the wine, bay leaf and seasoning, then add the mussels. Cook for about 5 minutes, or until the mussels open, stirring continuously. Discard any mussels that do not open.

5

Add the shrimps, tomatoes and capers to the pan, bring to the boil, then simmer gently for 2 minutes, stirring.

6

Add the tagliatelle and parsley and toss together to mix. Serve immediately.

Serving suggestion
Serve with warmed Ciabatta bread.

Variations
Use prawns or cockles in place of the shrimps. Use 4 shallots in place of the onion. Use a 400 g can chopped tomatoes in place of the fresh tomatoes.

Baked Lasagne with Meat Sauce

This classic *Lasagne al Forno* is ideal served with a fresh tomato salad.

Preparation time: 1 hour • Cooking time: 30-45 minutes • Serves: 4

Ingredients

14-16 sheets lasagne (approx. 250 g/9 oz)

15 ml (1 tbsp) olive oil

1 large onion, finely chopped

1 clove garlic, finely chopped

250 g (9 oz) mixed beef and pork mince

45 ml (3 tbsp) tomato purée

Salt and freshly ground black pepper

15-30 ml (1-2 tbsp) chopped fresh mixed herbs such as rosemary, oregano and thyme

200 g (7 oz) pot crème fraîche

125 ml (4 fl oz) milk

40 g (1½ oz) fresh Parmesan cheese, grated

40 g (1½ oz) butter

Method

1

Pre-cook the lasagne in a large saucepan of lightly salted, boiling water for 2 minutes, then rinse in cold water and drain thoroughly. Set aside.

2

Heat the oil in a saucepan, add the onion and garlic and cook gently for 10 minutes, stirring occasionally.

3

Add the meat mince, tomato purée, seasoning and herbs and add a little water, if necessary. Cover, bring to the boil and simmer for 30 minutes, stirring occasionally.

4

Mix the crème fraîche, milk and Parmesan cheese in a bowl and season to taste with salt and pepper.

5

To assemble the lasagne, lay a sheet of lasagne over the base of a lightly greased ovenproof dish. Add a layer of meat sauce, followed by another sheet of lasagne, followed by a layer of cream sauce.

6

Continue these layers until all the pasta and sauce are used up, ending with a layer of cream sauce.

7

Dot the butter over the surface and bake in a preheated oven at 200°C/400°F/gas mark 6 for 30-45 minutes, or until the top is golden brown and bubbling. Serve.

Serving suggestion
Serve with a fresh tomato salad and crusty French bread.

Variations
Use chicken and turkey mince in place of the beef and pork. Use 2 leeks in place of the onion. Use Cheddar cheese in place of the Parmesan cheese.

Carthusian-Style Crayfish Risotto

This delicious crayfish risotto is based on an original recipe used by Carthusian monks.

Preparation time: 20 minutes • Cooking time: 35-40 minutes • Serves: 6

Ingredients

500g (1 lb 2 oz) freshwater crayfish	*30 ml (2 tbsp) olive oil*
1 small onion, chopped	*1 clove garlic, crushed*
1 leek, sliced	*350 g (12 oz) risotto rice*
1 bay leaf	*1.2 litres (2 pints) fish stock*
1 sprig fresh parsley	*Salt and freshly ground black pepper*
115 g (4 oz) butter	*Fresh herb sprigs, to garnish*

Method

1

Place the crayfish in a saucepan with half the onion, leek, bay leaf, parsley and 850 ml (1½ pints) water. Bring to the boil and cook for 6-8 minutes. Drain thoroughly, then remove and discard the shells. Set the flesh to one side. Discard the vegetables.

2

Heat 55g (2 oz) butter and the oil in a large saucepan. Add the remaining onion and garlic and cook gently for 10 minutes, until softened, stirring occasionally.

3

Add the rice and cook for 1 minute, then add a ladleful of stock to the pan and cook gently, stirring frequently, until the stock is absorbed. Add more stock as soon as each ladleful is absorbed.

4

Continue adding stock, cooking and stirring until the rice becomes thick, creamy and tender. Stir in the crayfish and heat gently, stirring occasionally.

5

Stir in the remaining butter and seasoning, then serve immediately, garnished with fresh herb sprigs.

Serving suggestion

Serve with a chopped, mixed salad and warm fresh Focaccia bread.

Variations

Use fresh whole mussels or prawns in place of the crayfish. Serve the cooked, shelled crayfish on top of the cooked risotto, if preferred.

Risotto with Salmon

A risotto made with fresh salmon – ideal served as a quick family supper.

Preparation time: 15 minutes, plus 30 minutes standing time • Cooking time: 20 minutes • Serves: 4

Ingredients

400 g (14 oz) salmon steak, cut into bite-sized cubes	1 clove garlic, crushed
Juice of 1 lemon	125 ml (4 fl oz) white wine
30 ml (2 tbsp) vermouth	500 ml (18 fl oz) vegetable or fish stock
Salt and freshly ground black pepper	A pinch of saffron
55 g (2 oz) butter	200 g (7 oz) round-grained risotto rice
1 onion, finely chopped	30 ml (2 tbsp) chopped fresh parsley

Method

1

Place the salmon in a bowl and sprinkle over the lemon juice, vermouth and seasoning.
Set aside for 30 minutes, for the flavours to be absorbed.

2

Heat 25 g (1 oz) butter in a pressure cooker, add the onion and garlic and cook for 5 minutes, stirring.

3

Add the wine, stock, saffron, rice and seasoning, replace the lid, bring to pressure and cook for 8 minutes.

4

Release the steam quickly, remove the lid and add the salmon to the rice mixture. Cook for a further 5 minutes,
without the lid, until the salmon and rice are cooked, stirring occasionally.

5

Spoon the risotto onto a warmed serving plate, garnish with knobs of the remaining butter and
sprinkle with chopped fresh parsley. Serve.

Serving suggestion
Serve with a mixed leaf and cherry tomato salad.

Variations
Use other fresh fish such as tuna or smoked haddock in place of the salmon. Use red wine in place of the white wine.

Cook's tip
Risotto rice is a specific type of rice used to make classic Italian risotto dishes. It is a medium-grain rice
which can absorb up to 5 times its weight in liquid. White or brown risotto rice is available.

Sicilian Sardines

A popular and quick and easy dish to prepare, originating from the island of Sicily.

Preparation time: 15 minutes • Cooking time: 15 minutes • Serves: 4-6

Ingredients

800 g (1 lb 12 oz) fresh sardines	¼ green pepper, seeded and cut into thin strips
Salt and freshly ground black pepper	
30 ml (2 tbsp) lemon juice	1 clove garlic, crushed
30 ml (2 tbsp) plain flour	5 black olives
125 ml (4 fl oz) olive oil	5 green olives
1 small onion, sliced	15 ml (1 tbsp) chopped fresh parsley
¼ red pepper, seeded and cut into thin strips	15 ml (1 tbsp) chopped fresh oregano

Method

1
Season the sardines with salt and pepper, sprinkle with lemon juice, then coat them with flour.

2
Heat 100 ml (3½ fl oz) oil in a frying pan and cook the fish for about 10 minutes, or until cooked, turning occasionally. Remove from the pan and keep warm.

3
Add the remaining oil to the pan and heat gently. Add the onion, peppers and garlic and cook for 5 minutes, stirring occasionally.

4
Add the olives, parsley, oregano and seasoning and stir to mix.

5
Serve the sardines on warmed plates and spoon the onion mixture alongside.

Serving suggestion
Serve with hot, crusty garlic bread.

Variation
Use fresh pilchards or mackerel in place of the sardines.

Cook's tip
Olive oil is use widely in Italian cookery and is available in several grades, including extra virgin olive oil, which is the best quality olive oil. It is used in salad dressings and for drizzling over vegetables and salads, as well as for cooking.

Deep-Fried Seafood

A simple but delicious way to serve mixed seafood.

Preparation time: 15 minutes • Cooking time: 5 minutes • Serves: 4-6

Ingredients

4 small squid (about 400 g/14 oz)	*Vegetable oil, for deep-frying*
32 prawns in their shells	*Salt and freshly ground black pepper*
500 g (1 lb 2 oz) fresh sardines	*2 lemons, sliced or cut into wedges, to garnish*
Plain flour, for coating	*Shredded lettuce, to garnish*

Method

1

With larger squid, cut the body and tentacles into rings. Smaller squid can be left whole. Peel the prawns.

2

Coat the squid, prawns and sardines with flour and shake gently to remove any excess flour.

3

Heat the oil in a deep-fat fryer to 190°C/375°F. Lower the squid, prawns and sardines gently into the hot fat and deep-fry for 4-5 minutes, or until cooked, golden brown and crisp.

4

Remove from the pan using a slotted spoon and drain briefly on absorbent kitchen paper.

5

Place the cooked seafood on a warmed serving plate and season with salt and pepper.

6

Garnish with lemon slices or wedges and shredded lettuce and serve immediately.

Serving suggestion

Serve with thick slices of fresh crusty bread and a mixed pepper salad.

Variations

Use whitebait in place of the sardines. Add some chopped fresh mixed herbs to the flour.

Cook's tip

To peel prawns, grasp the head between finger and thumb and twist it to remove. Pull the legs to one side and in doing so, part of the shell should break away and lift off. Peel all the shell off.

Savoury Tuna Steaks

This flavourful tuna dish is ideal served with boiled rice or pasta for a filling meal.

Preparation time: 25 minutes • Cooking time: 7 minutes • Serves: 4

Ingredients

4 tuna steaks (each about 150 g/5½ oz)	125 ml (4 fl oz) white wine
30 ml (2 tbsp) sunflower oil	25 g (1 oz) butter
Juice of 1 lemon	4 tomatoes, skinned and sliced
55 g (2 oz) plain flour	Salt and freshly ground black pepper
45 ml (3 tbsp) olive oil	15-30 ml (1-2 tbsp) chopped fresh oregano
1 large onion, finely chopped	
1 clove garlic, crushed	Fresh herb sprigs, to garnish

Method

1
Fill the inner pan of a pressure cooker with 250 ml (9 fl oz) water. Brush the tuna steaks with the sunflower oil, sprinkle them with lemon juice, then toss them in flour. Shake gently to remove any excess flour.

2
Heat the olive oil in a frying pan and cook the fish until browned on both sides. Remove from the pan using a slotted spoon, cover and keep warm.

3
Add the onion to the pan and cook gently for 5 minutes, stirring occasionally.

4
Place the onion and garlic in the pressure cooker and lay the fish on top. Pour over the white wine.

5
In a separate pan, melt the butter, add the tomatoes and cook for 1 minute. Season with salt and pepper and stir in the oregano. Add the tomato mixture to the pressure cooker.

6
Seal the lid on the pressure cooker, bring to pressure and cook for 7 minutes. Release the steam quickly and remove the lid.

7
Spoon the tuna steaks and vegetables onto warmed serving plates and serve, garnished with fresh herb sprigs.

Serving suggestion
Serve with boiled fresh pasta, rice or noodles and seasonal fresh vegetables such as spring greens and cauliflower.

Variations
Use salmon steaks in place of the tuna. Use yellow or plum tomatoes in place of the standard tomatoes. Use chopped fresh marjoram or basil in place of the oregano.

Prawns in Garlic Butter

A simple dish to make that is hard to beat for a quick and tasty supper.

Preparation time: 10 minutes • Cooking time: 5 minutes • Serves: 4

Ingredients

30 ml (2 tbsp) butter	*Salt and freshly ground black pepper*
2-3 cloves garlic, finely chopped	*15-30 ml (1-2 tbsp) chopped fresh dill*
400 g (14 oz) cooked peeled prawns	*Lemon slices or wedges and fresh dill sprigs, to garnish*
30-45 ml (2-3 tbsp) dry sherry	

Method

1

Heat the butter in a saucepan, add the garlic and cook for 30 seconds.

2

Add the prawns, sherry and salt and pepper and stir to mix. Cover and cook for 5 minutes, stirring once or twice.

3

Stir in the chopped dill, then adjust the seasoning to taste.

4

Spoon the prawns onto a warmed serving plate.

5

Garnish with lemon slices or wedges and fresh dill sprigs and serve immediately.

Serving suggestion

Serve with crusty French bread or Italian Formaggio bread.

Variations

Use shelled cooked mussels or mixed seafood in place of the prawns. Use chopped fresh parsley in place of the dill.

Cook's tip

When buying garlic, choose plump, succulent bulbs with large cloves, which are bright and white in colour. The head of garlic should be firm, compact and not sprouting. Avoid soft, dark, mouldy, sprouting or shrivelled garlic.
If you don't have a garlic crusher, an easy way to crush garlic is to place the garlic clove under a heavy cook's knife with a wide blade and press down firmly to crush the garlic.

Chicken with Peppers

A flavoursome family chicken dish, ideal served with boiled new potatoes and seasonal fresh vegetables.

Preparation time: 25 minutes • Cooking time: 30 minutes • Serves: 4

Ingredients

1 chicken weighing about 1.5 kg (3 lb 5 oz)	*3 cloves garlic, crushed*
Salt and freshly ground black pepper	*3 large peppers, seeded and sliced*
60 ml (4 tbsp) olive oil	*4 large tomatoes, skinned and chopped*
1 onion, finely chopped	*Fresh herb sprigs, to garnish*

Method

1

Cut the chicken into four portions and remove and discard the skin. Season the chicken portions with salt and pepper.

2

Heat the oil in a frying pan, add the chicken portions and cook until browned all over, turning occasionally.

3

Remove the chicken from the pan using a slotted spoon and keep warm.

4

Add the onion, garlic, peppers and tomatoes to the pan and cook gently for 5 minutes, stirring occasionally.

5

Return the chicken to the pan and stir to mix. Cover and simmer for about 30 minutes, or until the chicken is cooked and tender, stirring occasionally.

6

Serve the chicken portions with the vegetables spooned over or alongside. Garnish with fresh herb sprigs.

Serving suggestion

Serve with boiled new potatoes and cooked seasonal fresh vegetables such as carrots and courgettes.

Variations

Use small turkey breast portions in place of the chicken. Use 2 leeks in place of the onion.
Use red, green or yellow peppers or one of each for this recipe.

Devilled Chicken

A delicious way to serve grilled chicken – ideal for barbecuing in the summer.

Preparation time: 25 minutes • Cooking time: 30-35 minutes • Serves: 4-6

Ingredients

2 chickens, each weighing about 1.5 kg (3 lb 5 oz)	*15-30 ml (1-2 tbsp) chopped fresh rosemary*
Salt and freshly ground black pepper	*30 ml (2 tbsp) olive oil*
Cayenne pepper, for seasoning	*Fresh herb sprigs, to garnish*
30 ml (2 tbsp) Dijon mustard	

Method

1

Cut along the backbone of each chicken with kitchen scissors and remove their backbones.

2

Flatten the chickens slightly using a cleaver or meat hammer. Season the insides and out with salt, black pepper and cayenne pepper.

3

Spread the mustard over the chicken and sprinkle over the rosemary.

4

Heat the oil in a large casserole dish and cook the chicken until browned on both sides, turning occasionally.

5

Place the casserole dish under a preheated medium grill and grill the chicken for 30-35 minutes, or until cooked and crispy, turning occasionally. Serve, garnished with fresh herb sprigs.

Serving suggestion

Served with sautéed potatoes and stir-fried mixed peppers and onions.

Variations

Use duck in place of the chicken. Use wholegrain mustard in place of the Dijon mustard. Use chopped fresh tarragon or thyme in place of the rosemary.

Cook's tip

Dijon mustard is a staple cooking mustard commonly used for dressings, sauces and coatings and it is an ideal partner for all meats. It is made from black or brown seeds which are blended with salt, spices and wine to create a creamy, yellow-grey coloured mustard with a clean, sharp, medium-hot flavour.

Hare in Tomato Sauce

This flavourful classic Italian dish can be prepared using rabbit if hare is not available.

Preparation time: 25 minutes, plus 24 hours marinating time • Cooking time: 2 hours • Serves: 4

Ingredients

1 hare, skinned and gutted	100 g (3½ oz) butterfat or lard
30 ml (2 tbsp) butter, melted	500 ml (18 fl oz) white wine
250 ml (9 fl oz) red wine vinegar	90 ml (6 tbsp) tomato purée
2 cloves garlic, finely chopped	75 ml (5 tbsp) olive oil
1 head celery, sliced	115 g (4 oz) streaky bacon, chopped
15 ml (1 tbsp) chopped fresh thyme	1.25 ml (¼ tsp) shredded bay leaves
Salt and freshly ground black pepper	60 ml (4 tbsp) brandy
Plain flour, for coating	Fresh herb sprigs, to garnish

Method

1

Clean the hare under running water, then cut it into portions and brush with melted butter.

2

Place the hare in a bowl or casserole dish, add the vinegar, 250 ml (9 fl oz) water, 1 clove garlic, celery, thyme and salt and pepper and stir to mix. Cover and leave in a cool place to marinate for 24 hours.

3

Remove the meat from the marinade using a slotted spoon. Discard the marinade. Dry the meat, then toss it in flour to coat all over.

4

Heat the butterfat or lard in a pan, add the hare portions and cook until the meat is browned all over, turning occasionally. Add a little wine and cook, stirring frequently, until the sauce thickens.

5

As the wine evaporates, gradually add more wine and continue cooking for 1½ hours, stirring frequently and adding more wine as it continues to evaporate and thicken.

6

Remove the meat from the casserole using a slotted spoon, cover and keep warm.

7

Add the tomato purée and any remaining wine to the pan and bring to the boil. Simmer for 5 minutes.

8

In a separate pan, heat the oil, add the bacon and cook until cooked and crispy, stirring.

9

Add the cooked bacon and bay leaves to the sauce and stir to mix. Finally, add the brandy to the sauce.

10

Place the cooked hare portions onto warmed serving plates and pour the wine sauce over. Serve immediately, garnished with fresh herb sprigs.

Serving suggestion

Serve with Italian Baked Potato Gratin (page 82) and cooked green beans.

Variations

Use rabbit in place of the hare. Use red wine in place of the white wine. Use smoked bacon for a tasty variation.

Rolled Escalope of Veal with Parma Ham

This delicious Italian veal dish is ideal served with sautéed or baked potatoes and char-grilled vegetables.

Preparation time: 15 minutes • Cooking time: 30 minutes • Serves: 4

Ingredients

4 escalopes of veal	55g (2 oz) butter
Freshly ground black pepper	30 ml (2 tbsp) olive oil
1 clove garlic, crushed	125 ml (4 fl oz) beef stock
8 fresh sage leaves	75 ml (5 tbsp) Marsala
4 slices Parma ham	Fresh herb sprigs, to garnish

Method

1
Lay the slices of veal flat on a board and season with black pepper. Rub the garlic over the meat.

2
Place 2 sage leaves and 1 slice of Parma ham on each escalope.

3
Roll up from the shortest side and secure with a wooden skewer or toothpick.

4
Melt 25 g (1 oz) butter in a frying pan with the oil. When hot, add the veal rolls and cook until the meat is browned all over, turning occasionally.

5
Add the beef stock, cover and bring to the boil. Reduce the heat and simmer gently for 15-20 minutes, or until the meat is cooked and tender, turning the meat occasionally.

6
Remove the meat from the pan using a slotted spoon, cover and keep warm.

7
Boil the sauce rapidly to reduce it, add the Marsala and reduce it further. Add the remaining butter to thicken the sauce and stir well to mix.

8
Cut the veal and ham rolls into slices, place on warmed serving plates and pour the sauce over. Serve, garnished with fresh herb sprigs.

Serving suggestion
Serve with sautéed or baked potatoes and char-grilled or oven-baked vegetables.

Variations
Use a little chopped fresh rosemary or thyme in place of the sage. Use prosciutto in place of the Parma ham.

Country-Style Casserole

This casserole makes a hearty family meal, served with herb-flavoured dumplings or potatoes.

Preparation time: 25 minutes, plus 12 hours marinating time • Cooking time: 2½ hours • Serves: 6

Ingredients

1 kg (2 lb 4 oz) braising steak, cut into 5-cm (2-in) slices	250 g (9 oz) pork belly, cut into small slices
500 ml (18 fl oz) white wine	4 carrots, sliced
30 ml (2 tbsp) brandy	2 onions, sliced
45 ml (3 tbsp) olive oil	250 g (9 oz) tomatoes, skinned and sliced
2 bay leaves	100 g (3½ oz) pitted black olives
4 cloves garlic, crushed	30 ml (2 tbsp) chopped fresh parsley
15-30 ml (1-2 tbsp) chopped fresh thyme	15 ml (1 tbsp) chopped fresh chives
Salt and freshly ground black pepper	15 ml (1 tbsp) chopped fresh rosemary
125 g (4½ oz) streaky bacon, cut into small slices	15 ml (1 tbsp) chopped fresh marjoram
	Chopped fresh parsley, to garnish

Method

1
Place the beef steak in a large, ovenproof casserole dish. Add the white wine, brandy, oil, bay leaves, garlic, thyme and seasoning and stir to mix.

2
Cover and leave in a cool place to marinate for 12 hours.

3
Add the bacon, pork belly, carrots, onions, tomatoes, olives and chopped herbs to the casserole and stir to mix.

4
Bake in a preheated oven at 180°C/350°F/gas mark 4 for about 2½ hours, or until the meat is cooked and tender, stirring once or twice.

5
Sprinkle with chopped fresh parsley and serve immediately.

Serving suggestion
Serve with herb-flavoured dumplings, boiled potatoes or noodles and a mixed pepper salad.

Variations
Use lamb in place of the beef steak. Use 3 leeks in place of the onions. Use parsnips in place of the carrots.

Saltimbocca of Calf's Liver with Risotto

A delicious risotto topped with tender, pan-fried calf's liver.

Preparation time: 25 minutes • Cooking time: 40 minutes • Serves: 6

Ingredients

120 ml (8 tbsp) olive oil	*750 g (1 lb 10 oz) calf's liver, cut into 12 equal slices*
1 onion, thinly sliced	*12 sage leaves*
1 clove garlic, thinly sliced	*12 slices Parma ham*
A pinch of saffron	*100 g (3½ oz) butter*
400 g (14 oz) risotto rice	*85 g (3 oz) fresh Parmesan cheese, grated*
1 litre (1¾ pints) beef stock	*Salt and freshly ground black pepper*

Method

1

Heat 45 ml (3 tbsp) oil in an ovenproof casserole dish. Add the onion and garlic and cook for 5 minutes, stirring.

2

Add the saffron and rice and cook for 1 minute. Add the stock and stir to mix.

3

Bring to the boil, then cover and bake in a preheated oven at 180°C/350°F/gas mark 4 for 30-40 minutes, or until the rice is cooked and tender.

4

Meanwhile, place the liver slices on a board and lay a sage leaf on each slice. Wrap each piece of liver in a slice of Parma ham and secure with a wooden skewer or cocktail stick.

5

Heat the remaining oil in a frying pan, add the liver and cook for 2 minutes on each side, turning once. Cover and keep warm.

6

Stir the butter and Parmesan cheese into the rice mixture and mix well. Season to taste with salt and pepper.

7

Spoon the risotto onto warmed serving plates and serve the liver on top of the rice.

Serving suggestion
Serve with a mixed leaf salad and warm Ciabatta bread.

Variations
Use lamb's liver in place of the calf's liver. Use basil leaves in place of the sage leaves. Use 4 shallots in place of the onion.

Liver with Sage

This quick and easy liver dish is flavoured with fresh sage. Dried sage may be used instead, but use fresh if you can, for maximum taste.

Preparation time: 20 minutes • Cooking time: 40 minutes • Serves: 6

Ingredients

115 g (4 oz) butter	*150 ml (¼ pint) white wine*
500 g (1 lb 2 oz) onions, chopped	*30-45 ml (2-3 tbsp) chopped fresh sage*
800 g (1 lb 12 oz) calf's liver, cut into thin strips	*45 ml (3 tbsp) chopped fresh parsley*
45-60 ml (3-4 tbsp) lemon juice	*Salt and freshly ground black pepper*

Method

1

Heat 55g (2 oz) butter in a pan, add the onion and cook gently for about 20 minutes, or until the onions are softened and golden yellow. Remove from the pan and keep warm.

2

Heat the remaining butter in the pan, add the liver and cook for about 5 minutes, or until the liver is cooked, stirring occasionally.

3

Remove the liver from the pan, place on a plate and sprinkle it with lemon juice. Cover and keep warm.

4

Add 100 ml (3½ fl oz) wine to the cooking juices in the pan and boil rapidly for 5 minutes.

5

Add the sage and onion and continue to cook for 5 minutes.

6

Add the liver, cook for a couple of minutes, then add the remaining wine and parsley and stir to mix. Heat briefly, season to taste with salt and pepper, then serve.

Serving suggestion

Serve with crusty French or country-style Italian bread.

Variations

Use lamb's liver in place of the calf's liver. Use leeks in place of the onions. Use red wine in place of the white wine.

Tuscan-Style Lamb

A tasty lamb roast, ideal for warming chilly winter days.

Preparation time: 25 minutes • Cooking time: 1½ hours • Serves: 6

Ingredients

500 g (1 lb 2 oz) canned chopped tomatoes	12 cloves garlic, peeled
Salt and freshly ground black pepper	90 ml (6 tbsp) olive oil
10-15 ml (2-3 tsp) dried rosemary	500 g (1 lb 2 oz) frozen peas
1 kg (2 lb 4 oz) leg of lamb	

Method

1
Purée the tomatoes in a blender or food processor, then pour them into a saucepan.

2
Bring to the boil, then simmer for 5 minutes. Stir in salt, pepper and rosemary and set aside.

3
Make 12 slashes in the lamb at intervals, then push the garlic cloves into the slashes.

4
Heat the oil in an ovenproof casserole dish, add the lamb and cook until browned all over, turning occasionally.

5
Add the tomato mixture to the casserole and stir to mix.

6
Cover and bake in a preheated oven at 180°C/350°F/gas mark 4 for about 1½ hours, or until the lamb is cooked and tender.

7
Add the peas, stir to mix, then cook for a further 10 minutes. Serve.

Serving suggestion
Serve with baked potatoes and seasonal fresh vegetables such as broccoli and cauliflower florets.

Variations
Use beef topside or pork leg in place of the lamb. Use broad beans in place of the peas.

Italian Vegetable Casserole

A sumptuous combination of Italian-style vegetables, ideal served with fresh crusty bread.

Preparation time: 15 minutes • Cooking time: 40 minutes • Serves: 4

Ingredients

45 ml (3 tbsp) olive oil	*4 beefsteak tomatoes, skinned and sliced*
1 onion, sliced	*45 ml (3 tbsp) tomato purée*
2 cloves garlic, crushed	*15 ml (1 tbsp) chopped fresh basil*
1 green pepper, seeded and sliced	*15 ml (1 tbsp) chopped fresh thyme*
1 red pepper, seeded and sliced	*15 ml (1 tbsp) chopped fresh marjoram*
300 g (10½ oz) courgettes, sliced	*salt and freshly ground black pepper*
250 g (9 oz) aubergines, sliced	*30 ml (2 tbsp) chopped fresh parsley*

Method

1

Heat the oil in a large saucepan. Add the onion and garlic and cook for 5 minutes, stirring.

2

Add the peppers, courgettes and aubergines and cook for 5 minutes, stirring occasionally.

3

Add the tomatoes, tomato purée, basil, thyme, marjoram and 200 ml (7 fl oz) water and stir to mix. Season with salt and pepper.

4

Cover, bring to the boil, then simmer for about 30 minutes, or until the vegetables are cooked and tender, stirring occasionally.

5

Transfer to a warmed serving dish and sprinkle with chopped fresh parsley before serving.

Serving suggestion

Serve with fresh crusty bread or baked potatoes, topped with melted cheese.

Variations

Use 8 plum tomatoes in place of the beefsteak tomatoes. Use sun-dried tomato purée, for a tasty change.

Cook's tip

Use dried herbs if fresh are not available. Use approximately 5 ml (1 tsp) dried herbs to every 15 ml (1 tbsp) fresh herbs.

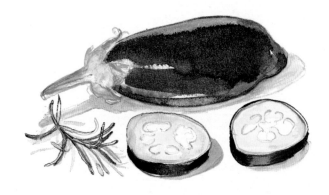

Country-Style Artichokes

An inviting way to serve artichokes, ideal as an appetising accompaniment to meat dishes.

Preparation time: 20 minutes • Cooking time: 40 minutes • Serves: 4

Ingredients

8 small globe artichokes	10 ml (2 tsp) tomato purée
90 ml (6 tbsp) olive oil	150 ml (¼ pint) vegetable stock
300 g (10½ oz) onions, finely chopped	100 g (3½ oz) olives
2 cloves garlic, finely chopped	10 ml (2 tsp) capers
Salt and freshly ground black pepper	

Method

1
Prepare the artichokes. Cut off the stalks and remove a few of the rough outer leaves with scissors, ensuring that all the brown or dried edges are removed. Set aside.

2
Heat the oil in a flameproof casserole dish. Add the onions and garlic and cook for 10 minutes, or until softened, stirring occasionally.

3
Add the artichokes and seasoning and cook for 10 minutes, stirring occasionally.

4
Add the tomato purée and stock and stir to mix.

5
Bring to the boil and simmer for 10 minutes, stirring occasionally.

6
Add the olives and capers and simmer for a further 10 minutes, stirring occasionally. Serve.

Serving suggestion
Serve with grilled or pan-fried meat or fish such as lamb cutlets or salmon steaks.

Variations
Use 10 ml (2 tsp) garlic purée in place of the fresh garlic. Use shallots in place of the onions. Use chicken or beef stock in place of the vegetable stock.

Cook's tip
To make a quick and delicious home-made vegetable stock, simply place a selection of prepared fresh vegetables such as onions, carrots, swede, parsnips and celery in a saucepan with some black peppercorns and fresh herb sprigs. Cover with plenty of water, bring to the boil, then simmer for 1½ hours, skimming occasionally. Strain the stock and use as required.

Roman Courgettes

Serve this richly flavoured dish with crusty bread to mop up the juices.

Preparation time: 30 minutes • Cooking time: 20-25 minutes • Serves: 4-6

Ingredients

15 ml (1 tbsp) olive oil	*Salt and freshly ground black pepper*
55 g (2 oz) streaky bacon, diced	*500 g (1 lb 2 oz) courgettes*
1 onion, finely chopped	*30 ml (2 tbsp) plain flour*
1 clove garlic, finely chopped	*60-75 ml (4-5 tbsp) chopped fresh mixed herbs*
500 g (1 lb 2 oz) tomatoes, skinned and chopped	*40 g (1½ oz) fresh Parmesan cheese, grated*
15 ml (1 tbsp) chopped fresh oregano	*90 ml (6 tbsp) crème fraîche*

Method

1

Heat the oil in a saucepan, add the bacon and cook until browned all over, stirring.

2

Add the onion and garlic and cook for 5 minutes, stirring.

3

Add the tomatoes, oregano and seasoning and stir to mix. Bring to the boil, then cook gently for about
15 minutes, or until the sauce thickens slightly, stirring occasionally.

4

Cut each courgette in half lengthways and sprinkle with a little salt.

5

Mix the flour, herbs, Parmesan cheese and crème fraîche together and coat the courgette halves with this mixture.
Place them in a shallow ovenproof dish and pour the tomato sauce over.

6

Bake in a preheated oven at 220°C/425°F/gas mark 7 for 20-25 minutes, or until the courgettes are cooked and tender. Serve.

Serving suggestion

Serve with fresh crusty bread and a chopped mixed salad.

Variations

Use small aubergines in place of the courgettes. Use one 400 g (14 oz) can chopped tomatoes
in place of the fresh tomatoes. Use chopped fresh basil in place of the oregano.

Cook's tip

For the fresh mixed herbs, use parsley, oregano and rosemary or a mixture of herbs of your choice.
Alternatively, use 10-15 ml (2-3 tsp) dried mixed herbs in place of the fresh herbs.

Sicilian Broccoli

Fresh broccoli florets oven-baked with a piquant sauce.

Preparation time: 20 minutes • Cooking time: 1½ hours • Serves: 6-8

Ingredients

55 g (2 oz) pitted black olives, sliced	250 ml (9 fl oz) olive oil
8 anchovy fillets, thinly sliced	Salt and freshly ground black pepper
1 small onion, finely chopped	2 kg (4 lb 8 oz) broccoli florets
55 g (2 oz) fresh Parmesan cheese, grated	300 ml (½ pint) dry red wine

Method

1
Place the olives, anchovies, onion and Parmesan cheese in a bowl and stir to mix.

2
Add 200 ml (7 fl oz) oil and mix well. Season to taste with salt and pepper.

3
Spoon a little oil mixture over the base of a lightly greased, shallow, ovenproof dish. Cover with a layer of broccoli florets.

4
Cover the broccoli with a little more oil mixture and top with broccoli florets.

5
Continue these layers, until all the oil mixture and broccoli are used up, finishing with a layer of broccoli.

6
Drizzle the remaining oil over the top and pour the wine over the vegetables.

7
Cover with foil and bake in a preheated oven at 170°C/325°F/gas mark 3 for about 1½ hours,
or until most of the wine has been absorbed. Serve.

Serving suggestion
Serve with hot buttered toast, warm Ciabatta bread or baked potatoes.

Variations
Use 2 shallots in place of the onion. Use a mixture of broccoli and cauliflower florets in place of all broccoli. Use Cheddar cheese in place of the Parmesan cheese.

Italian Baked Potato Gratin

An easy recipe to make and a delicious one to enjoy served with grilled meat or fish.

Preparation time: 15 minutes • Cooking time: 1 hour, 5 minutes • Serves: 10

Ingredients

10 large floury potatoes	*55 g (2 oz) butter*
Salt	*Freshly ground black pepper*
125 ml (4 fl oz) milk	*55 g (2 oz) fresh Parmesan cheese, grated*
125 ml (4 fl oz) double cream	

Method

1
Wash the potatoes and cut a slice off the top of each of them lengthways. Sprinkle lightly with salt.

2
Place the potatoes on a lightly greased baking sheet and bake in a preheated oven at 200°C/400°F/gas mark 6 for 40 minutes.

3
Cool slightly, then hollow out the potatoes, using a spoon and taking care not to damage the skins.

4
Place the potato flesh in a bowl, add the milk, cream, butter and black pepper and mix well.

5
Spoon the potato mixture back into the potato skins and place them on the baking sheet.
Sprinkle the potatoes with Parmesan cheese.

6
Bake in a preheated oven at 200°C/400°F/gas mark 6 for 25 minutes, until golden brown and bubbling. Serve.

Serving suggestion

Serve with gilled meat such as steak or lamb chops and a mixed pepper and tomato salad.

Variations

Add 45-60 ml (3-4 tbsp) chopped fresh mixed herbs to the potato mixture. Use crème fraîche in place of the cream. Use Cheddar cheese or crumbled blue cheese such as Dolcelatte in place of the Parmesan cheese. Pipe the potato mixture into the potato shells, for a more decorative effect.

Baked Spinach

Cheesy-topped baked spinach makes a delicious starter or accompaniment to pan-fried fish.

Preparation time: 20 minutes • Cooking time: 15-20 minutes • Serves: 6

Ingredients

1 kg (2 lb 4 oz) fresh spinach leaves	*150 g (5½ oz) Mozzarella cheese, diced*
90 ml (6 tbsp) olive oil	*90 ml (6 tbsp) finely grated fresh Parmesan cheese*
1 clove garlic, crushed	
45 ml (3 tbsp) pine nuts	*Salt and freshly ground black pepper*

Method

1
Remove and discard any thick, tough stems from the spinach. Wash and drain the spinach leaves thoroughly.

2
Drizzle some oil over the base of a baking tin and scatter the garlic over the top.

3
Spread the spinach evenly over the top and press down lightly. Drizzle with the remaining oil.

4
Scatter the pine nuts over the spinach and top with the Mozzarella cheese.

5
Sprinkle with Parmesan cheese and season with salt and pepper.

6
Bake in a preheated oven at 220°C/425°F/gas mark 7 for 15-20 minutes, or until the spinach is cooked and the cheese is melted and bubbling. Serve.

Serving suggestion
Serve with crusty Italian bread or pan-fried fish or poultry such as cod steaks or chicken breasts.

Variations
Use spring greens or kale in place of the spinach. Use Cheddar cheese in place of the Parmesan cheese. Use finely chopped nuts such as hazelnuts or walnuts in place of the pine nuts.

Cook's tip
Choose small, young and tender spinach leaves which are fresh and bright in colour. Avoid thick, woody steams. Baby spinach leaves are widely available and are ideal and delicious.

Cassata

This luxury dessert uses Amarena cherries which are preserved in syrup, becoming candied but juicy with a natural dark red colour. They smell of bitter almonds.

Preparation time: 30 minutes, plus freezing time • Serves: 6

Ingredients

400 g (14 oz) cherry ice-cream

30 ml (2 tbsp) Maraschino (Italian cherry liqueur)

300 g (10½ oz) almond and caramel ice-cream

30 ml (2 tbsp) cracknel

300 g (10½ oz) vanilla ice-cream

55 g (2 oz) Amarena cherries, chopped

Whipped cream and Amarena cherries, to decorate

Method

1

Place a cake or pudding mould in the freezer for 1 hour.

2

Press the cherry ice-cream against the sides of the mould using a spatula, then brush the Maraschino over the ice-cream. Freeze for 30 minutes.

3

Press the almond and caramel ice-cream over the cherry ice-cream and sprinkle with the cracknel. Freeze for 30 minutes.

4

Finish by mixing the vanilla ice-cream with the Amarena cherries and pressing this over the other ice-creams in the mould, filling the mould completely. Freeze for 1 hour.

5

Plunge the mould briefly in a bowl of hot water and turn out onto a chilled plate. Decorate with rosettes of piped cream and Amarena cherries. Serve immediately in slices.

Serving suggestion

Serve with wafer biscuits and fresh cherries.

Variations

Use chocolate or coffee ice-cream in place of the vanilla ice-cream. Use cocktail cherries if Amarena cherries are not available.

Peaches in Meringue

A simple yet impressive fruit dessert.

Preparation time: 15 minutes • Cooking time: 15 minutes • Serves: 6

Ingredients

850 g (1 lb 14 oz) canned peaches, drained	*25 g (1 oz) ground almonds*
25 g (1 oz) butter	*30 ml (2 tbsp) orange-flavoured liqueur*
1 egg white	*25 g (1 oz) chopped almonds*
55 g (2 oz) caster sugar	*or mixed nuts*

Method

1
Place the peaches in a shallow, ovenproof dish. Melt the butter and pour it over the peaches.

2
Place the dish under a preheated grill and grill for 5 minutes.

3
Remove from the heat, turn the peaches over in the butter and grill for a further 5 minutes.

4
Meanwhile, whisk the egg white in a bowl until stiff. Fold in the sugar, a spoonful at a time, until it is all incorporated.

5
Fold in the ground almonds, then carefully fold in the liqueur.

6
Spoon the mixture over the peaches and sprinkle with chopped almonds or mixed nuts.

7
Place under the grill for 4 minutes, until lightly browned. Serve.

Serving suggestion
Serve with crème fraîche, Greek yogurt or cream.

Variations
Use other canned fruit such as apricots or pears in place of the peaches. Use ground hazelnuts in place of the almonds. Use light soft brown sugar in place of the caster sugar.

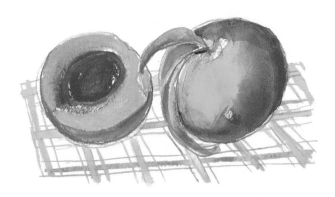

Date and Fig Sorbet

An appetising sorbet which makes an ideal treat at the end of any meal.

Preparation time: 30 minutes, plus freezing time • Cooking time: 10-15 minutes • Serves: 6

Ingredients

100 ml (3¹/₂ fl oz) rosewater

55 g (2 oz) caster sugar

45 ml (3 tbsp) honey

3 egg whites

55 g (2 oz) toasted flaked almonds

115 g (4 oz) mixed crystallised fruits, finely chopped

250 ml (9 fl oz) whipping cream

*115 g (4 oz) plain chocolate,
broken into squares*

55g (2 oz) chopped mixed nuts

12 fresh dates, peeled, stoned and halved

3 fresh figs, halved

Method

1
Place the rosewater in a saucepan with the sugar and heat gently until the sugar has dissolved.

2
Bring to the boil and simmer gently until the mixture forms a thick syrup. Stir in the honey and remove from the heat.

3
In a bowl, whisk the egg whites until stiff. Place the bowl over a pan of simmering water and slowly add the hot syrup to the egg whites, whisking continuously, until the mixture becomes stiff.

4
Fold in the toasted almonds and crystallised fruits.

5
Whip the cream in a separate bowl until stiff, then fold into the egg white mixture.

6
Spoon the mixture into a rectangular mould and freeze until firm.

7
Plunge the mould briefly into a bowl of hot water and turn out onto a board. Cut the dessert into slices and then into strips and return to the freezer. Freeze until firm.

8
Melt the chocolate in a bowl placed over a pan of simmering water.

9
Stir in the chopped nuts, then dip one end of each strip of frozen sorbet into the chocolate mixture, to decorate.

10
Decorate with the fresh dates and figs and serve immediately.

Serving suggestion
Serve with thin wafer biscuits.

Variations
Serve with other fresh fruits, such as mixed berries or pineapple, in place of the dates and figs. Use maple syrup in place of the honey.

Tiramisu

This popular Italian dessert creates a mouth-watering finale to any meal.

Preparation time: 25 minutes, plus 2 hours chilling time • Serves: 6

Ingredients

30 ml (2 tbsp) drinking chocolate powder

3 medium eggs, separated

60 ml (4 tbsp) honey

300 g (10½ oz) Mascarpone cheese or crème fraîche

One 20 cm (8 in) pre-baked sweet shortcrust pastry flan case

15 ml (1 tbsp) cocoa powder

Extra cocoa powder, to decorate

Method

1

In a bowl, blend the chocolate powder with 200 ml (7 fl oz) hot water. Set aside to cool.

2

Place the egg yolks and honey in a bowl and beat together until they are frothy.

3

Add the Mascarpone cheese or crème fraîche and beat together to mix.

4

In a separate bowl, whisk the egg whites until stiff. Fold in the cheese mixture carefully but thoroughly.

5

Spread ⅓ of the mixture over the base of the flan case. Sprinkle with the cold chocolate mixture and sift 15 ml (1 tbsp) cocoa powder over the top.

6

Spread the remaining cheese mixture evenly over the top. Chill in the refrigerator for 2 hours.

7

Dredge with sifted cocoa powder to decorate and serve in slices.

Serving suggestion

Serve with fresh fruit such as strawberries or raspberries.

Variations

Use cream cheese in place of the Mascarpone cheese. Use carob powder in place of the cocoa powder.

Florentines with Wine and Date Cream Sauce

A delicious dessert that is bound to impress your dinner guests every time.

Preparation time: 45 minutes, plus chilling and setting time • Cooking time: 20 minutes • Serves: 12

Ingredients

175 g (6 oz) plain flour	200 g (7 oz) flaked almonds
A pinch of salt	5 fresh dates, peeled, stoned and finely chopped
140 g (5 oz) butter, chilled	
175 g (6 oz) granulated sugar	15 ml (1 tbsp) powdered gelatine
1 medium egg, beaten	100 ml (3½ fl oz) white wine
30 ml (2 tbsp) honey	30 ml (2 tbsp) caster sugar
400 ml (14 fl oz) double cream	12 fresh dates, peeled, stoned and halved

Method

1
Sift the flour and salt into a bowl. Add 100g (3½ oz) butter, 85g (3 oz) granulated sugar and egg and knead the ingredients together to form a smooth dough. Wrap and chill for 2 hours.

2
Roll the dough out thinly on a lightly floured surface and cut into twelve 10-cm (4-in) rounds. Place the rounds on baking sheets lined with greaseproof or non-stick baking paper.

3
Place the remaining butter, remaining granulated sugar and honey in a pan and heat gently until beginning to caramelise. Stir in 125 ml (4 fl oz) cream and cook gently, stirring, until the mixture thickens.

4
Stir in the almonds and chopped dates and set aside to cool.

5
Once cool, spoon the mixture into heaps on the pastry rounds. Bake in a preheated oven at 200°C/400°F/gas mark 6 for 20 minutes, or until golden brown.

6
Leave to cool for a few minutes on the baking sheets, then transfer to a wire rack to cool completely.

7
Meanwhile, make the sauce. Sprinkle the gelatine over 45ml (3 tbsp) water in a small bowl and leave to soak for a couple of minutes.

8
Pour the wine into a saucepan, add the gelatine and heat gently until the gelatine has dissolved, stirring. Cool the pan in a bowl of cold water.

9
Whisk the remaining cream with the caster sugar, until stiff.

10
Whisk in the wine mixture, then set aside in a cool place to set.

11
Once the wine mixture starts to set, pipe the mixture over the cooked, cold pastries, to decorate. Place half a date on the top of each pastry and serve.

Serving suggestion
Serve with fresh mixed fruit salad.

Variation
Use rose wine in place of the white wine.

Index